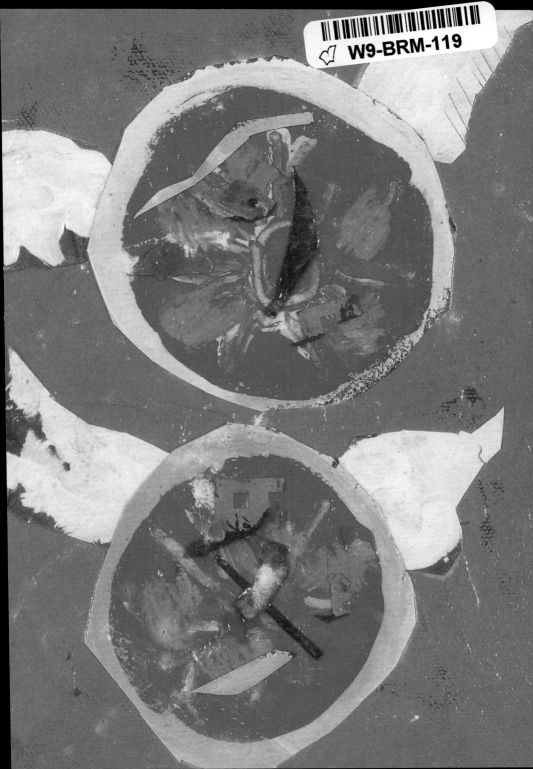

the raw food primer

THE RAW FOOD PRIMER

CHEF SUZANNE
ALEX
FERRARA

council oak books / san francisco and tulsa

Acknowledgments

Walking through a bookstore, I now understand that every book I see represents an astonishing amount of energy and love. The people we love, like a village standing strong behind us, challenge us to be great. I want to thank my village for its unfailing support. Thank you, Felicity. You rule. Thank you, Mimi, Laurel, and Kristina, for the early days. The first little booklet was a rainy day project that gathered momentum. Thank you, Jules, for believing in and feeding this baby. Yes, it goes on and on. Mom, Dad, Jerry, Amy, Kelly, Dotty, Tamara, Chad, Roxanne, Cheri, Terri, Lambie, everyone who bought those early pamphlets, everyone who came to the classes and dinners. Of course, Bob. And Patrice, thank you for keeping me funny.
—Chef Alex

Designer: Carol Haralson
Editor: Carol Haralson
Illustrations: Chef Suzanne Alex Ferrara

I S B N 1-57178-130-7

Council Oak Books, LLC
2105 East Fifteenth Street, Suite B
Tulsa, Oklahoma 74104
918.743.BOOK
800.247.8850

Einstein was a vegetarian.

the raw food primer

why raw?

my raw life

I began this journey thirty years ago when it became obvious to me that my constitution would not allow me to eat a standard American diet. As a young woman, I was already experiencing serious health problems. I went to doctors and took their pills but continued to be sick. Several raw food eaters came through my life at this time. They were exceptionally clear and beautiful beings, and I aspired to be the same. While I read books, it wasn't the books that convinced me; it was my own food experiments. In less than a year, I transformed myself into a new person: body, mind, and spirit. My own brother did not even recognize me.

I have always loved food preparation. As a child I read cookbooks and was comfortable taking on complex recipes. I was enchanted by the everyday magic of delighting people with taste. It was inevitable that I would take what I knew about traditional foods and translate those experiences into the raw language. As an artist I saw the opportunity to make my offerings edible paintings. I took my knowledge of texture and balance and created a rich raw food cuisine.

I encourage everyone to try uncooking, not only because it is healthy and tastes better, but also because it inspires a deeper connection to yourself, others, and the planet. I have used this method of eating as a tool. These days I eat only raw, but for more than twenty years I danced in and out of the practice. Eating raw food was a therapy, not a way of life. But, gradually, the periods of time I was raw took over. I noticed that my body was functioning on a high nutritional level, and that cooked food had become difficult for me to enjoy. After eating a raw meal, one feels energized, alert, and happy instead of sleepy, dull, and sedated. Eating raw is eating for your life.

A fully raw diet is not for everyone—but fresh fruits and vegetables certainly are, and this book can stimulate your imagination as to how you can add more of them to your diet in a fun and sensual way. When it comes to improving your health, it is a tortoise and hare race. The slow and steady approach brings success. The road is long, so enjoy the scenery.

raw food

A raw food diet of uncooked fruits, vegetables, nuts, and seeds is about intense nutrition. When the temperature of food is raised above 118 degrees, enzymes die and vitamins can be depleted. Since digestion depends on enzymes, the body must produce these lost enzymes in order to process food. Cooking food is an inefficient method of fueling ourselves; it wastes energy and makes us old before our time. Fortunately, the body is a forgiving organism that, nourished properly, will rejuvenate. Eating uncooked food allows the body to cleanse itself, bringing about the healing of chronic conditions, as well as a euphoric sense of well-being.

As with most things, there are variations in the uncooked theme: Life Food, Live Food, Natural Hygiene, and Fruitarianism, to name a few. A purist will eat what is known as mono meals—one kind of fruit on an empty stomach until full. I agree that eating just an apple is an elegant concept, but not something easily done on a regular basis. If you eat a standard diet of cooked food, meat, and dairy and wish to go raw, you must change gradually. Eat one raw meal a day for a month, two raw meals a day the next month, and so on. The body is a self-cleaning machine. Eating uncooked food can eliminate excess weight and accumulated toxins as you get out of the way of the body's cleaning process. Opening the door to regeneration is easier than you think, but detoxification takes time.

Raw foodists have been called "the thin people," but this is not necessarily true. People in the early stages of this eating style commonly lose weight, but after living the raw life for some time, their bodies seek their natural weight.

Eating is social communion as well as one of life's more profound pleasures. With the blossoming of raw food as an artistic cuisine, its practitioners are rediscovering the intensity of natural flavors and enticing high palate food lovers to explore a once exclusively health-oriented way of eating. As raw food enters the culinary mainstream, innovative minds have surfaced to create dishes that conform to the principles and standards of high nutrition and give the satisfying comfort of traditional cuisines. In order to be completely nourished, you must love your food. You can go on an austere regimen, but the day you succumb to your emotional traditions will be your undoing. My plan is to create something new that embraces our sensual beings while supporting our vitality. Love your food!

II

going raw

food combining Different types of food have different digestion times. Simply combining foods properly will make digestion more efficient. This improvement alone will visibly change you and prepare you for the next shift. (Read *Food Combining Made Easy,* by Herbert Shelton)

going vegetarian Carnivorous animals have short digestive tracts so that meat can pass through them quickly. The human digestive tract is longer so meat moves through it more slowly, taking more energy to digest. That's one reason people choose to be vegetarian, and there are others. Being vegetarian means that you do not eat meat. This means fish, too. (Read *Diet for a New America,* by John Robbins)

going vegan Next on the scale is the elimination of animal products other than meat from one's diet. Dairy foods can coat the digestive track with a substance forcing your system to work harder and hindering the absorption of vital nutrients. Once they discontinue dairy products, many people discover that they no longer have allergies. Using nut milks and cheeses, you can rediscover some of your old favorite foods without the congestion that accompanies dairy products, while you spare consumer dairy animals the cruelty of high-yield, profit-driven practices. (Read *Bragg Healthy Lifestyle,* by Paul Bragg and Patricia Bragg)

half raw A half raw diet will sustain a moderate cleanse. The transition to a higher energy diet should be done gently. One hundred percent, highly charged, live food will break toxins loose very quickly, but this cleansing work is best done in increments. A raw diet sensitizes your system, allowing you to become aware of foods that make you feel bad, and you will know it is time forego these foods when they disagree with you. Many health benefits will be experienced just by eating a 50 to 75 percent raw diet. (Read *Surviving into the 21st Century*, by Viktoras Kulvinskas)

raw I don't have a stove in my kitchen. When people visit me, I serve them raw foods. We have raw pancakes, cream cheese, apple pie, and even sandwiches. My guests never feel deprived, and I can keep even most omni-food eaters happy for a while. The food most people eat is so challenging to natural digestion that even the smallest improvement is rewarded by smoother skin, leaner structure, and clearer eyes. But becoming 100 percent raw without a transitional diet can be both physically and mentally challenging. Pay attention to what your body is saying by detoxifying gradually as you add more raw meals to your diet. (Read *Conscious Eating*, by Gabriel Cousens)

are there worlds beyond raw? The next time you have a cold, conduct this experiment: for one whole day, eat only fruit. Choose one type per meal, and eat until you are full. The next day, eat as you normally would. Notice the difference in your suffering. A fruit diet supports cleansing. Some people eat this way all the time. I have enjoyed very tranquil retreats on an all-fruit diet. Meditation comes easily and the body is miraculously limber, making for exceptional yoga. However, I choose to live in a world where I can be in the kitchen and prepare food with my family and friends. In meditation, I have learned why high yogis do not need food, but I have also come to understand that the gift of nourishing others is a spiritual path as well.

the raw pantry

STOCK UP YOUR BASIC RAW FOOD PANTRY at the farmer's market, health food store, organic section of your supermarket, online, or from your own garden or windowbox. Then add a variety of vibrant fruits and vegetables in tune with the season, and you're set to uncook!

almond butter (raw): If you have a Champion Juicer or another machine that homogenizes, you can make and store fresh almond butter from raw, organic almonds. If you don't want to or cannot make your own, a good choice is Maranatha Organic Raw Almond Butter. If your health food store does not carry it, you can order it from Sun Organic Farms.

almonds: Raw, organic almonds are indispensable. The dark outer skin of the almond acts as an enzyme inhibitor that slows down the sprouting cycle. This enzyme inhibitor also slows the enzymatic action necessary for our digestion. Soak almonds for six or more hours to lower oil content as well as optimize digestibility.

apple cider vinegar: Buy only raw, organic apple cider vinegar, such as Braggs, available at most health food stores.

basil: Fresh is always best. When basil is plentiful, freeze it, or dry it by leaving it in a warm place. Crumble and store it in an airtight container.

black pepper: Use only freshly milled pepper; once cracked, it loses flavor and can turn rancid.

carob powder (raw): Carob powders are not created equal. Raw is available, but if the carob pods have not been milled to a fine powder the result is gritty. If your source has this gritty variety, re-mill it in a coffee grinder or a Vita Mixer.

cashews: The process of removing the outer layers of the cashew nut often involves excessive heat so they are not considered raw, although I have had cashews that sprouted.

cayenne: Besides making everything a bit sassy, this powdered hot pepper has amazing health benefits. The brighter the red, the fresher the grind.

cilantro: Fresh cilantro has no substitute. Dried cilantro is flat and will not work in these recipes.

cinnamon: I have a little army of coffee/spice grinders, one devoted to cinnamon. Freshly ground cinnamon stick gives a euphoric lift. It is so much more delicious than commercially powdered cinnamon they can hardly be compared.

coconut: Purchase unpasteurized, unsulfured, shredded organic coconut at your local health food store. I use a coffee or spice mill to grind flour from shredded coconut.

cumin: A romancer of taste buds, this seed is a digestive aid as well. Grind it fresh, and store it in a small airtight container.

curry powder: There are more than twenty possible ingredients in the spice mix we know as curry powder. In India, I enjoyed the seemingly endless varieties of curry. Create your own mix using cardamom, cayenne, celery seed, coriander, cumin, fenugreek, garlic, ginger, onion, and turmeric.

dates: My favorite date is the organic medjool. Be aware that a cooking process has been used in preparation of date paste, date rolls, and pitted dates.

flaxseed: This highly beneficial seed has a gelatinous quality that binds during dehydration. I prefer golden flax for its color but the traditional dark brown variety works equally well. Always buy flaxseed in its whole state as it is highly perishable, and for the price of one jar of ground flax you can invest in a coffee/spice mill and grind your own. Seeds and nuts do not turn rancid as quickly if stored whole.

garlic: Fresh is best, although I occasionally use a powdered version when preparing food for garlic-sensitive diners. Removing the center green sprout is also helpful for garlic sensitives.

ginger: Organic ginger root is difficult to find; when you do, store it in the freezer. It grates well while frozen.

honey: Raw, unfiltered honey is one of the most enzyme-rich foods available. However, some vegans shun it as an animal product; you can make up your own mind.

maple sugar: Maple sugar is granulated sugar made from maple syrup. While it is not a raw product, it makes an excellent sweetener and can be purchased in organic form.

maple syrup: Maple syrup is not raw, but is a natural sweetener acceptable for strict vegans.

miso: This thick, salty paste is made from soybeans, grains, and sea salt. It is a live food when unpasteurized. I prefer mellow, white miso made by Miso Master.

nama shoyu: Aged in wooden kegs, traditional, unpasteurized Japanese soy sauce is a fermented, live food, lower in salt than other soy sauces or tamari. The Ohsawa brand is available through most health food stores. Nama means "raw."

nutmeg: Grate it fresh.

olive oil: Buy only organic, cold pressed olive oil, and keep it stored in a cool, dark place.

oregano: Grow your own in the summer, then freeze or dry it for winter.

pecans: Soak to break down enzyme inhibitors and lower the oil content. See the Quick Guide, page 25.

pine nuts: Also called pignoli or piñons, pine nuts come from the pine cone of the piñon tree. They are highly perishable and should be stored frozen. They do not require soaking unless a recipe specifically calls for it.

prunes: Buy only organic prunes.

pumpkin seeds: Buy only raw, organic pumpkin seeds.

raisins: I prefer organic Thompson raisins.

sea salt: Unrefined sea salt has a damp, gray appearance. Avoid white, processed table salt. It is not water-soluble and contains many objectionable ingredients. I once had dinner in a restaurant where a salt tasting from around the world was one of the courses.

It's amazing how different salts are, in taste and in color. Gray Celtic sea salt from the Northwest coast of France is particularly prized for its trace element and mineral content, and it is my favorite. The word "Celtic" refers to the method of its harvesting, in which it is neither washed nor boiled. Most importantly, choose sea salt over standard table salt for purity and solubility.

sunflower seeds: Recipes call for hulled, raw, organic sunflower seeds.

tahini (organic): A butter made from raw sesame seeds.

walnuts: Soak before using; see the Quick Guide, page 25.

water: The chemical soup that comes from the faucet is not appropriate for discerning recipes. It is best to use distilled water.

resources

dehydrators

Mountain Home Basics
2535 D. Rd
Grand Junction, CO 81503
Tel 800.572.9549
www.dehydrators.com

They carry three models. The small one (Excalibur model 2400) is available for just under $100. Tell Steve you saw it here, and you'll get free shipping in the continental U.S. Don't forget to order Teflex sheets.

dried snacks

Glaser Organic Farms
www.glaserorganicfarms.com
Tel 305.238.7747

Blessings Alive
www.powerfood.org
Tel 415.482.7788

nut milk bags

www.purejoylivingfoods.com
Tel 831.338.1104

nuts, seeds, and other stuff

Sun Organic Farm
www.sunorganic.com
Tel 888.269.9888

Living Tree Community Foods
www.livingtreecommunity.com
Tel 510.420.1440

organic produce

Diamond Organics
www. diamondorganics.com
Tel 888.ORGANIC
P.O. Box 2159, Freedom, CA 95019

raw chefs/training

Chef Chad Sarno
www.rawchef.org

The Boutenko family
rawfamily@home.com
Tel 541.488.8865

Chef Cherie Soria
Living Light
www.rawfoodchef.com
Tel 800.816.2319

Chef Suzanne Alex Ferrara
www.chefsuzannealexferrara.com

tools

RAW CUISINE DEPENDS ON PREPARATION rather than cooking, so every tool you acquire brings new depth to your raw meals. To begin, get a blender and juicer. A dehydrator is the next important basic. These need not be the most expensive or recent models. A small Excalibur dehydrator can be had for around $100 (see resources, page 19). Or try garage sales or newspaper ads for reasonably priced juicers, mixers, dehydrators, and food processors. Expand your toolkit whenever you have the chance and your options for creating expressive raw cuisine will expand along with it.

blenders and mixers: Almost any blender will make soups, sauces, and salad dressings. But for the smoothest textures, use a Vita Mixer.

coffee grinders and spice mills: Standard small coffee grinders are perfect for milling flours and powdering spices.

dehydrators: The type of dehydrator you purchase is a deciding factor in what you will be able to create in your kitchen. I use the Excalibur dehydrator, which seems made for raw foodists. This machine is like an oven in that you can warm things with it. It is also front-loading. This allows you want to make long, flat sheets, which round dehydrators make impossible. The Excalibur also has a heat gauge, an option many others leave out.

I always leave my dehydrator set at 105 degrees. A few years ago, there was quite a stir about drying temperatures. I had the opportunity to test many different types of food while dehydrating with a digital probe thermometer. I concluded that the actual temperature of the food was a great deal lower than the surrounding air in a dehydrator. I was satisfied.

dehydrator sheets: Two types of dehydrator sheets are available with an Excalibur dehydrator. One is a solid sheet known as a Teflex sheet. It has to be ordered separately. It is made with Teflon, so wash it gently to avoid scratching it. Foods with a high liquid content are dried on a solid sheet. Many things start out on the Teflex sheet but end up on perforated sheets. Perforated sheets come with the dehydrator.

food processors: I have three of these because I like having different sized bowls. When I travel, I take a smaller Oskar with me and work in batches when necessary, but the Cuisinart is my favorite. It stands up to the heavy work of nut and seed pulverizing and can process large batches. The Cuisinart is indispensible. You might as well name yours because it will soon be your best friend.

graters, zesters, spatulas, ice cream scoopers, strainers . . . : The more tools, the merrier. Consider these items as essential as carpenter's tools.

juicers: The Champion Juicer is the one you'll love. It can make nut cheeses using the homogenizing option and can turn frozen bananas and smoothie ice cubes into ice cream, a favorite trick with this versatile machine. Be sure to keep the shaft oiled (I use coconut butter) to avoid getting the blade nose stuck. Store disassembled.

Small electric juicers meant for citrus fruit are great for a quick glass of freshness, but be sure to have a hand juicer around too for small tasks like reaming a lemon or orange.

knives: Buy yourself a good one (perhaps German), keep it clean, keep it sharp, and don't let anyone else use it.

molds, pans, and formers: Terrine molds, springform pans, and vertical food formers of all all sizes and shapes are great for high-art presentations.

spiralizer: The spiralizer, or spiral slicer, is a little manual gadget that can cut zucchini into capellini-like noodles. It is ingenious. Spiralizers are available through most cooking stores. Mine is by Joyce Chen Eastern Cookware for Western Kitchens. Many raw food websites, as well as mine, sell them.

water distiller: I know it won't come as a surprise to you that water is not getting any better. Filter systems are Band-Aids. Invest in a high-quality water distillation or reverse osmosis system. You can't keep piling up those plastic jugs by the back door forever.

quick guide

dehydrating

The dehydrator is not a necessary companion to raw food living, but it is a luxury you should allow yourself if you want to explore this diet. Excalibur makes a variety of temperature controlled dehydrators that start at about $100 (see Resources). However, it is possible to use the sun to achieve a version of some recipes that call for a dehydrator. When my daughter was away at school she found that she could make lovely cookies and croquettes on a plate over her heating vent. Even the open air of your refrigerator has a drying affect. A few recipes, such as cereal and crackers, call for bone-dry results, so these are best made in a thermostat controlled dehydrator. In general, you should start the dehydrating process on a solid dehydator sheet to avoid a mess in the dehydrator. When one side is dry enough to be semi-solid, you can flip the food onto its other side on a perforated sheet and continue drying. This speeds the drying process.

about time

Related to the question of dehydrating is the question of time. I've heard more than once that it takes too much time to prepare raw meals. Actually, although the process of dehydration may take many hours, the active preparation time for many raw food recipes is less than in traditional cooking. The trick is to think differently about time, and to get into the habit of thinking ahead. I like to designate one day a week as food prep day— it may be just a couple of hours on Sunday afternoon. I'll make some sauces, a nut cheese, a soup broth, marinated vegetables, and some crackers or a bread. You can also pre-soak nuts in large batches to have on hand. I like to keep a dessert in the freezer so I have something flashy to offer company.

reheating

In the winter it is nice to have warm food. Leave food out of refrigeration to bring it to room temperature or place it on a plate over a bowl of hot water. Some soups are made with heated water. Never heat beyond what is comfortable for your finger and never microwave.

go organic

Fruits, vegetables, nuts, and seeds in my recipes are always organic. Buying organic is voting for a better planet. You can make a difference while treating your palate to the finest taste available.

soaking nuts

Nuts (except pine nuts) and seeds for all the recipes that follow are always pre-soaked and drained.

Soaking makes them easier to digest and lowers their oil content. Nuts should soak for at least six hours over overnight. If you want them crunchy you can re-dry them in the dehydrator after soaking. You can soak nuts for longer periods if you keep them in the refrigerator and change the water daily. You can pre-soak nuts in large batches so they are recipe-ready.

Nut butters, such almond butter, are available at health food stores. Read the labels carefully to be sure you are getting a raw, unsalted product.

use sea salt

Salt in my recipes is always sea salt. Celtic is best due to the great care taken to preserve its trace elements and minerals

use pure water

Use only purified or distilled water.

breakfast

food processor
dehydrator

This nutty mixture, with its comforting texture, makes a superb cereal. Add almond milk (page 87) for a powerful way to start the day. Enjoy it as a topping, too. It lends a sweet, seductive crunch to many dishes.

1 cup almonds
1/2 cup pecans
1/2 cup walnuts
1 cup sunflower seeds
2 cups water
1/2 cup maple sugar

1 cup golden flaxseed
2 cups water
1/3 cup maple syrup
1/2 teaspoon
cinnamon
two pinches of salt

makes 4 cups

Soak almonds, pecans, walnuts, and sunflower seeds in 2 cups water for 6 to 8 hours. Rinse, drain, and chop coarsely. Toss the nut and seed mixture in a bowl with the maple sugar and a pinch of salt. Dehydrate at 105 degrees for seven hours. Set aside.

Soak flaxseed in 2 cups water for 4 hours, then drain it and place it in a food processor with the maple syrup, cinnamon, and pinch of salt. Process for several minutes to make a batter. Spread the batter very thinly on solid dehydrator sheets. Dry 3 hours. Turn the batter over and place it on perforated dehydrator sheets. Continue drying until it is completely crispy. Crumble into small flakes. Mix these flakes with the dehydrated nut and seed mixture. Store in the freezer.

crunchy nut cereal

food processor
or Vita Mixer
dehydrator

Place the pear, walnuts, pine nuts, maple syrup, water, cinnamon, and vanilla in a food processor or Vita Mixer and blend to make a completely smooth batter.

Pour silver-dollar-sized rounds out onto solid dehydrator sheets. Dehydrate 6 hours. Flip, then dehydrate another 6 hours.

Serve with maple syrup and fresh fruit.

1 ripe pear

1 cup soaked walnuts

1 cup pine nuts

1/3 cup maple syrup

1/4 cup water

1 teaspoon cinnamon

1/2 teaspoon vanilla

This is not your everyday breakfast. Serve these pancakes to company or on special holidays.

makes about 12 pancakes

pear-walnut pancakes

spice grinder

blender

2 tablespoons flaxseed

1 whole, ripe mango

1/2 tablespoon maple syrup

1/4 teaspoon vanilla

pinch of nutmeg

lemon zest

serves 2

Powder the flaxseed in a spice grinder. Peel and seed the mango and place it in a food processor with the powdered flaxseed, maple syrup, vanilla, and nutmeg. Process until completely smooth.

Pour into martini glasses and chill for at least 30 minutes.

Top with lemon zest and serve.

This is a favorite breakfast of mine. I like to serve this puddling to little girls at tea parties. Elegant glasses are a must.

mango pudding

soups

This cool and creamy sensation calms the nerves as it soothes the stomach. It is the perfect light meal for summer heat. The almond milk provides some serious nutrition without the bulk.

blender

Place the cucumber, celery, cilantro, garlic, almond milk, brazil nuts, miso, and cumin in a blender. Blend until creamy.

Pour into bowls and garnish with freshly cracked black pepper and snipped chives.

1 medium cucumber, peeled and minced

1 cup minced celery

1 tablespoon minced fresh cilantro

1 teaspoon minced garlic

1 cup almond milk (page 87)

6 soaked brazil nuts

1 tablespoon white miso

1/4 teaspoon ground cumin

black pepper

chives

serves 2

creamy cucumber soup

blender

2 cups almond milk (page 87)
2 cups minced celery
1 cup fresh spinach, packed
2 tablespoons white miso
2 teaspoons olive oil
2 teaspoons minced garlic
pinch of cayenne
1/2 cup corn kernels
7 sun-dried olives, pitted
lemon zest

serves 2

Place almond milk, 1 cup of the celery (reserve the other cup), spinach, miso, olive oil, garlic, and 4 olives (reserve and mince the remaining 3), in a blender and blend. Pour into 2 bowls.

Divide the remaining cup of minced celery and the reserved minced olives between the bowls. Sprinkle the corn so that it floats enticingly on the surface of the soup. Garnish lightly with lemon zest. Dust both bowls with cayenne and serve. Cheers!

cream of spinach soup

34

Once, while traveling in New Mexico, I had a restaurant experience that left me struggling to create a raw meal from what was offered on the menu. After managing to get some lettuce and an avocado, I was left with an abundance of salsa. After eating the entire bowl intended for chips, I mused: Now, that's one great gazpacho! This is my interpretation.

Combine all the ingredients in a glass bowl and serve.

1-1/2 cups seeded and diced Roma tomatoes

1 cup carrot juice

1 cup tomato juice

1/2 cup minced red bell pepper

1/2 cup minced celery

1/2 cup peeled and minced zucchini

1/2 cup minced white onion

1/4 cup seeded and minced sweet yellow pepper

1/4 cup lemon juice

2 tablespoons shoyu

1 tablespoon minced fresh oregano

1 tablespoon minced fresh basil

2 teaspoons honey

2 teaspoons lime juice

1 teaspoon chili powder

1 teaspoon minced fresh thyme leaves

1 teaspoon onion powder

1/2 teaspoon ground cumin

1/4 teaspoon cayenne

freshly cracked black pepper

serves 4

gazpacho

blender

1 whole, ripe avocado

2 cloves garlic

3 tablespoons shoyu

1/8 teaspoon ground cumin

1 teaspoon fresh lime juice

warm water

Peel the avocado and and remove the pit. Place the flesh in a blender with the garlic, shoyu, cumin, and lime juice. Blend, adding small amounts of warm water until the consistency is that of thick soup. The amount of water will vary from avocado to avocado but generally will be about one cup.

sweet red bell pepper

Sliver or chop the red bell pepper and scatter atop the soup as a garnish.

serves 1

> This rich, velvety soup will make you feel extraordinary and will compel you to smile continuously for hours. It has a buttery essence that can smooth out the rough edges of any winter day.

avocado heaven

36

blender

1 cup cubed portobella mushroom (scrape away the black feathers)

1 cup peeled and minced zucchini

1/4 cup minced red bell pepper

1/2 cup finely minced carrots

1/2 cup minced fresh cilantro

1/4 cup minced tomato

2 tablespoons olive oil

1 tablespoon shoyu

1 cup warm water

2 tablespoons miso

2 tablespoons almond butter

1 to 2 garlic cloves

cayenne, optional

serves 2

Place the mushroom, zucchini, red pepper, carrots, cilantro, tomato, olive oil, and shoyu in a bowl.

Place the water, miso, almond butter, and garlic in a blender and blend until smoothly combined.

Stir the miso–almond butter mixture into the fresh vegetable mixture.

Divide the soup between two bowls, and serve with a dash of cayenne, if you like.

Each bite of this soup is a flavorful explosion. Its beauty is exceeded only by the force of its energy—vibrant energy. It makes you feel downright electric. Plug in.

miso mushroom soup

blender

Place the tomatoes, sunflower seeds, zucchini, shoyu, honey, basil, and garlic in a blender and blend until smooth and creamy, adding enough purified water to keep the mixture turning easily.

Garnish with chopped parsley

3 medium tomatoes, chopped
1/2 cup soaked sunflower seeds
1/2 cup chopped zucchini
3 tablespoons shoyu
1 tablespoon honey
1 teaspoon fresh basil
3 garlic cloves
water

parsley

serves 2

This simple and elegant soup is made with the vine-ripened lovelies from your own tomato garden. Quickly, invite the Caraway Crackers (page 73) to this meal. They're great companions!

real tomato soup

blender

3 cups chopped tomatoes

2 cups warm water

1/2 cup sun-dried tomatoes soaked in 1/2 cup water for 30 minutes or more

1/4 cup shoyu

1 tablespoon almond butter

1 tablespoon maple syrup

1 teaspoon fresh oregano

1 teaspoon fresh thyme

1/4 teaspoon cayenne

1/2 cup minced zucchini

1/2 cup fresh corn kernels

1/2 cup fresh peas

1/2 cup pine nuts

1/4 cup minced white onion

yellow bell pepper matchsticks

serves 4

Place the fresh tomatoes, water, sun-dried tomatoes with their soaking water, shoyu, almond butter, maple syrup, oregano, thyme, and cayenne in a blender and blend until smooth.

Remove the mixture to a bowl and add the minced zucchini, corn kernels, peas, pine nuts, and onion. Fold in by hand.

Divide into bowls and garnish with pepper matchsticks.

I eat this hearty stew on many chilly evenings. It reminds me of homemade minestrone soup from my childhood.

vegetable stew

40

sauces + dressings

Place all the ingredients in a glass jar with a tight-fitting lid and shake to combine. Refrigerate.

1/2 cup apple cider vinegar

1/2 cup olive oil

1/4 cup shoyu

5 tablespoons honey

1 teaspoon garlic powder

1 teaspoon minced fresh thyme

1 teaspoon minced fresh ginger

1/8 teaspoon cayenne

makes about 1-1/4 cup

When I go to restaurants, I take this dressing with me in a little leak-proof camping bottle. Of course, I often I have to share, since it is usually far better than what is offered.

sweet and sour ginger dressing

43

Place all the ingredients in a blender and blend until smooth. Store refrigerated in a glass container.

1 cup chopped tomato

1/2 cup fresh grapefruit juice

1/2 cup olive oil

1/4 cup minced carrot

1/4 cup minced celery

2 tablespoons apple cider vinegar

3 pitted dates

2 cloves garlic

2 teaspoons poppyseeds

1/2 teaspoon sea salt

makes 1-1/2 cup

This lively pink dressing is especially good with young spinach leaves.

grapefruit dressing with poppyseeds

45

blender

1 cup carrot juice
4 tablespoons almond butter
1/2 ripe avocado, peeled and pitted
2 tablespoon shoyu
1 teaspoon garlic powder
1 teaspoon honey

makes 1-1/4 cup

Put carrot juice, almond butter, avocado, shoyu, garlic powder, and honey in a blender and blend until smooth. If the mixture becomes too thick to turn easily, add a small amount of purified water.

This sauce was invented for Raw Raviolis (page 60) but you can dream up other good uses for it. When serving it with a dish like the ravioli, spread the sauce on a plate first, then top with the ravioli. This presentation will be more than spectacular. Supply a soup spoon for dishes served with this sauce as it is good to the last drop.

carrot almond sauce

blender

1 cup sun-dried tomatoes soaked in
1 cup water until soft (about 30
minutes), with their soaking water

1 cup chopped fresh tomatoes

1/2 cup chopped carrot

3 tablespoon olive oil

2 tablespoons minced fresh oregano

2 tablespoons shoyu

1 teaspoon fresh rosemary

1/2 teaspoon fresh thyme

1 to 2 cloves garlic

makes 2 cups

Many people find the quality of this sauce equal to the familiar marinara cooked by traditional means. Remarkably, it takes only minutes rather than the whole day required to prepare a classic marinara sauce.

Combine all the ingredients in the blender and blend until smooth.

marinara

47

blender

1 cup warm water

1 cup minced celery

1/2 cup sun-dried tomatoes, soaked 30 minutes or more in 1/2 cup water, with their soaking water

1/2 cup minced parsley

1/3 cup almond butter

1/4 cup minced white onion

1/4 cup shoyu

3 pitted dates

2 garlic cloves

1 teaspoon minced fresh rosemary

1 teaspoon chili powder

1/4 teaspoon cayenne

makes 3 cups

This dreamy, Southern-style gravy will take on any vegetable plate, elevating it to the highest levels within comfort-food zones. Try it with Faux Meat Loaf (page 52). Leftover gravy will thicken, making a pleasing cracker spread.

Place all the ingredients in a blender and blend until creamy and smooth. The gravy keeps well in the refrigerator.

red-eye gravy

48

entrées

Eggplant Tacos

food processor
dehydrator

Peel the eggplant, slice it into very thin rounds, and sprinkle with sea salt. Place in the dehydrator at 105 degrees or in a hot, sunny window to soften. Softening time will vary from a few minutes to just less than an hour, depending on the thickness of the slices. They are ready to stuff when you can fold them without their sides splitting.

Place the walnuts, celery, onion, zucchini, water, garlic, shoyu, chili powder, cumin, and oregano in a food processor and blend until creamy.

Stuff the filling into the eggplant slices and fold each one in half to make tacos. Dehydrate for 2 to 12 hours, as desired. Store in airtight container in the refrigerator.

1 eggplant
sea salt

1 cup soaked walnuts
1/2 cup chopped celery
1/4 cup minced white onion
1/2 cup chopped zucchini
1/4 cup water
2 cloves garlic
3 tablespoons shoyu
1 teaspoon chili powder
1/2 teaspoon ground cumin
1/2 teaspoon minced fresh oregano

serves 4 as an entrée

This is the ultimate snack food. Not only does it travel well, but its savory depth pleases even the most difficult-to-coerce traditional food eaters. Good soft and warm, but also divinely intense when completely dry. This dehydrator food has many lives—I continue to experiment with all stages, from warm to bone dry.

eggplant tacos

food processor

dehydrator

1/2 cup soaked walnuts

1/2 cup soaked almonds

1/2 cup chopped carrots

1/2 cup minced portobella mushroom

1/2 cup chopped celery

1/2 cup minced onion

1/2 cup sun-dried tomatoes, soaked in 1/2 cup water for 30 minutes or more, with their soaking water

1/4 cup pine nuts

2 tablespoons almond butter

2 tablespoons minced garlic

1 tablespoon white miso

1 tablespoon shoyu

1 tablespoon fresh oregano

1 teaspoon dried thyme

1 teaspoon chili powder

makes 5 small loaves

When the need for nostalgic comfort food arises, this will be your best choice. These little loaves are great with Red-Eye Gravy (page 48).

Put all the ingredients in a food processor and process to combine—but stop before the mixture is completely smooth. Texture should be chunky. Line a loaf pan with plastic wrap and mold the mixture in the pan. Refrigerate overnight.

Using the plastic wrap, lift the loaf from the pan and place it on a cutting board. Cut it into 5 smaller loaves and wrap each one individually.

The loaves may be refrigerated or frozen. To serve, slice each small loaf into 3/4-inch servings. If frozen, warm them in the dehydrator or a sunny window for 2 hours.

faux meat loaves

52

Peel the whole zucchinis and make them into "noodles" using a potato peeler to make long, flat strips that you can then slice lengthwise into perfect noodle shapes. Set them aside.

Blend all the remaining ingredients in a blender until they form a smooth sauce. Toss the sauce with the zucchini "noodles." Garnish with chopped bell peppers and cracked pepper. Serve immediately.

2 whole zucchinis

1/2 cup soaked cashews
1/2 cup almond milk (page 87)
1/2 cup peeled and minced zucchini
1/2 cup pine nuts
2 tablespoon olive oil
1 teaspoon minced garlic
1 teaspoon fresh oregano
2 teaspoons white miso
chopped red or yellow sweet bell peppers, for garnish
freshly cracked black pepper

serves 2

There is a bit of sculpture involved in making this dish. The thinner the noodles, the more authentic the experience. Be sure to peel the green completely off the zucchini. Experiment with different kitchen tools—my favorite is the potato peeler, but you may find your own favorite.

fettuccini alfredo

1 cup freshly cut corn kernels

1/2 cup minced red bell pepper

1/2 cup diced celery

1/2 cup pine nuts

1/2 cup minced yellow onion

1 large tomato, cut into chunks

1 tablespoon olive oil

1 tablespoon shoyu

1 tablespoon grated lemon rind

1 teaspoon apple cider vinegar

1 teaspoon minced garlic

1/2 teaspoon ground cumin

1/2 teaspoon dried thyme

radicchio leaves

serves 4

Mix all the ingredients together in a bowl. Wash and separate the leaves of one or more heads of radicchio, depending on size. Fill each leaf with a scoop of the corn and pepper filling. It's best to do this at the last moment so the leaves will not wilt, or present the filling in a decorative bowl with crisp leaves on the side and let diners roll their own.

> The colors combined in this dish are so jewel-like they will make you want to take up painting.

festive radicchio rolls

54

Peel eggplant and slice into very thin rounds.

Sprinkle with sea salt. Place in the dehydrator at 105 degrees for 30 minutes. Mince the portobella mushroom. Combine the onion powder, olive oil, shoyu, water, and thyme in a bowl and add the mushrooms. Allow to marinate.

Spoon Marinara Sauce over each eggplant slice, then top with olives, onion, oregano, and the marinated mushroom mixture. Dust with sea salt and onion powder. Accent with thin bell pepper strips. Dehydrate for 3 to 4 hours. You can dry these in a sunny window, but the truly airborne pizzas are from the dehydrator.

> You may not actually see the wings on your pizzas, but I promise you they will fly—right out of your dehydrator. I recall one particular dinner party where guests hovered in the kitchen, afraid to leave the pizzas unguarded. The number of people this will serve depends largely on your appetite for sacrifice.

1 eggplant
1 large portobella mushroom
1/2 teaspoon onion powder
2 tablespoons olive oil
1 tablespoon shoyu
1 tablespoon water
1/2 teaspoon dried thyme

Marinara Sauce (page 47)
sun-dried olives, cut in half and pitted (2 per pizza)
1/4 cup white onion slivers
minced fresh oregano
sea salt
onion powder
1/4 cup red bell pepper slivers

serves 4 as an entrée

flying eggplant pizzas

nut butter machine or juicer
capable of homogenizing nuts

food processor

slicer or mandoline

1 cup soaked macadamia nuts

1 cup water

1 tablespoon mellow white miso

1 tablespoon fresh oregano

1/2 tablespoon onion powder

3 to 5 cloves garlic

2 teaspoons thyme

1/2 teaspoon sea salt

1/2 cup minced fresh spinach

1 large zucchini

sun-dried tomatoes for garnish

Marinara Sauce (page 47)

makes about 20 roll-ups

Homogenize the macadamia nuts. Place the resulting nut butter, water, miso, oregano, onion powder, garlic, thyme, and salt in a food processor and process until smooth. Pulse in the spinach.

Slice the zucchini into paper-thin strips about 4 inches in length. Spoon a tablespoonful of nut mixture onto each zucchini "manicotti" strip and roll it up. Store the roll-ups standing on end in the refrigerator until ready to serve.

Even your Italian mother-in-law will love this dish. It can be prepared up to a day in advance, and it makes a nice companion for the Sicilian Caponata. Paint a plate with Marinara Sauce and top it with the Manicotti Bites and minced sun-dried tomatoes.

manicotti bites with marinara and sun-dried olives

Toss all the ingredients except the endive leaves together in a large bowl. Warm the mixture in the dehydrator and then spoon it into endive leaves. Garnish with more endive, fresh oregano, and cracked black pepper.

Traditionally, caponata is lightly sautéed. The slight softening of the vegetables and the marrying of the spices is mimicked in the raw version by placing the mixture on a solid dehydrator-warming sheet for 1 to 2 hours at 105 degrees. The caper berries are soaked in distilled water to lessen their salt and vinegar content.

1 cup cubed zucchini

1/2 cup minced celery

1/2 cup minced white onion

1/2 cup tomatoes, cut into chunks

7 sun-dried olives, minced

2 tablespoons capers, soaked in distilled water and drained

2 tablespoons olive oil

2 to 3 minced garlic cloves

1 tablespoon shoyu

1 tablespoon minced fresh oregano

1 teaspoon dried thyme

endive leaves, separated

serves 4

sicilian caponata with endive leaves

59

food processor

1 cup soaked walnuts

1 cup chopped zucchini

3 tablespoons shoyu

2 cloves garlic

1 teaspoon fresh oregano

1/2 cup minced red onion

1/2 cup minced celery

1/4 cup minced red bell pepper

wilted butter lettuce leaves

Carrot Almond Sauce (page 46)

serves 3

Put the walnuts, zucchini, shoyu, garlic, and oregano in a food processor and process until creamy. Remove to a bowl and fold in the onion, celery, and red bell pepper by hand.

Leave large lettuce leaves out of the refrigerator long enough to wilt. Remove heavy center vein. Place 1 tablespoon of filling on each leaf and roll to wrap up tight. Serve with Carrot Almond Sauce.

When they thoroughly wilt, butter lettuce leaves take on an elastic quality that keeps them from tearing as you wrap the raviolis. These scrumptious little pillows will enchant any diner. Arrange the raviolis on a platter painted with rich Carrot Almond Sauce.

raw raviolis

60

Croquettes with Red-Eye Gravy and avocado slices make a beautiful presentation. Or—instead of dehydrating the croquette batter, enjoy it as pâté in lettuce leaves.

juicer

food processor

dehydrator

Place the carrot pulp (pulp left over from making carrot juice) in the food processor with the pine nuts, water, almond butter, shoyu, garlic, thyme, and cumin and blend until smooth. Remove the mixture to a bowl. Mince the mushroom and fold it into the mixture by hand with the peas.

Shape into palm-sized patties and place on a solid dehydrator sheet. After 2 hours remove to a perforated sheet. Dehydrate at 105 degrees for 2 to 4 more hours. (Croquettes can also be dried in a sunny window.) Serve with Red-eye Gravy and avocado slices.

2 cups carrot pulp

1 cup pine nuts

1/2 cup water

1/4 cup almond butter

1/4 cup shoyu

3 to 5 cloves garlic

1/2 teaspoon thyme

1 teaspoon ground cumin

1 medium-sized portobella mushroom

1/2 cup peas, frozen (freezing and thawing fresh peas softens them)

avocado

Red-Eye Gravy (page 48)

serves 4

carrot croquettes

63

3 tablespoons olive oil

1 tablespoon shoyu

1/2 teaspoon minced garlic

1/2 teaspoon dried thyme

1 tablespoon water

1/2 teaspoon ground cumin

1/2 cup sliced portobella mushrooms

Seed Bread (page 70)

avocado

lettuce

sliced tomato

makes 2 to 3 sandwiches

Combine the olive oil, shoyu, garlic, thyme, water, and cumin in a bowl. Add the portobella slices and allow to marinate 10 minutes.

Assemble the mushroom slices on pieces of seed bread and top with avocado, lettuce, and sliced tomato.

This deceptively simple sandwich is also quite good rolled in a romaine lettuce leaf. Try it with Marinated White Onion Rings (page 74) too.

the mlt
[mushroom, lettuce, and tomato sandwich]

64

food processor
blender
dehydrator

1/2 cup soaked sunflower seeds
1 medium carrot, chopped
1 medium zucchini, chopped
2 garlic cloves
2 tablespoons shoyu
1 fresh basil leaf

2 tablespoons tahini
2 tablespoons mellow white miso
1 garlic clove
1 teaspoon dried thyme
water
minced carrot, red pepper and
parsley

serves 4

Place the sunflower seeds, carrot, zucchini,
garlic, shoyu, and basil in a food processor
and process until smooth. Form the
mixture into 4 patties and dehydrate for 5
hours.

Put the tahini, miso, garlic, and thyme in a
blender and blend, adding water slowly to
achieve gravy consistency. Ladle gravy onto
a plate. Arrange the croquettes over the
gravy and garnish with a confetti of minced
carrots, red bell pepper, and parsley.

Use this recipe as a jumping-off point to create your
own croquettes. In my cooking school, I like to
emphasize concept dishes. Use what you have on
hand, e.g., substitute nuts for seeds, and vary the
vegetables, using the same proportions as the
original recipe.

sunflower croquettes
in tahini gravy

bread, condiments + little bites

Remove the rind from the lemons and cut it into
small chunks. Retain the pith, or white, of the
rind, as it has health benefits. The honey will
offset its bitterness. Place the chunks in a jar with
a sprinkling of cinnamon. Add enough honey to
cover all the rind. Allow the rind to infuse for at
least 3 hours.

Store in the refrigerator.

It keeps indefinitely.

organic lemons

honey

cinnamon

In the winter, these little candies are like
bursts of sunshine. It is incredibly
satisfying to make something fabulous out
of what most people throw away. The
honey preserves the rind so it is always
ready in your refrigerator to be a child's
treat or the bright spot on your dinner
plate. You may wish to sprinkle the rind
with freshly grated nutmeg before serving.
Nice with any seasonal fruit.

honey infused lemon rind

69

spice grinder

food processor dehydrator

1 cup hulled sunflower seeds ground into meal using a spice or coffee grinder

2 cups flaxseed

3 cups water

1 cup flax meal (made by grinding flaxseed in a spice or coffee grinder)

21/2 cups water

1/3 cup shoyu

1 tablespoon onion powder

makes 13 rolls

This seed bread is a breakthrough in the sandwich department. Once you get this recipe down, your sandwiches will be the house specialty.

Put the 1 cup ground sunflower seeds in a bowl with the 2 cups flaxseed and add the 3 cups of water. Soak overnight (seeds will absorb all the moisture so there will be no need to drain).

Put the flax meal and the soaked seed mixture in a food processor along with the water, shoyu, and onion powder. Process several minutes to thoroughly combine into a mostly smooth dough. Form the dough a half-cupful at a time into thirteen sandwich rolls and place them on a solid dehydrator sheet. Dehydrate 6 hours on each side. As they dry, you can flatten them and continue to make small adjustments to their shape.

Slice each roll in half and dehydrate for 1 hour more. Store the rolls in the refrigerator in a loosely covered container (refrigerator continues a moderate dehydration.)

seed bread

70

nut butter machine or
juicer capable of
homogenizing nuts

2 cups soaked cashews
1 tablespoon white miso
2 tablespoons water
1/4 teaspoon sea salt

makes about 2-1/2 cups

Homogenize the cashews through the juicer or nut butter homogenizer (my choice is the Champion Juicer with the nut butter plate in place). Thoroughly blend with miso, salt, and water. Cover and let stand in a warm place for 6 to 8 hours. Refrigerate.

I consider this cashew cream cheese a kitchen staple. Once you have had it, you won't want to live without it. Enjoy it with crackers, veggies, stuffed mushrooms, and lots more.

cashew cream cheese

food processor

dehydrator

Soak the flaxseed in 2 cups of water for at least 5 hours or overnight. The seeds will absorb all the water.

Place the soaked flaxseed in a food processor with the carrot pulp, shoyu, garlic powder, caraway seed, and water. Process several minutes. Stop the machine, scrape down the sides, and turn the mixture by hand, then continue processing several more minutes.

Spread the mixture thinly on solid dehydrator sheets and dry for 3 hours. Flip over onto perforated sheets, score into desired cracker sizes, and continue to dehydrate until crispy, about 6 to 8 hours. Store in a cool dry place.

2 cups flaxseed

2 cups water

2 cups carrot pulp

1/2 cup shoyu

1 tablespoon garlic powder

1 tablespoon caraway seed

1/2 cup water

makes 3 13-inch squares

Use this recipe as a model for your own flaxseed creations.
Add your favorite spices and your best imagination.

caraway crackers

1 or more white onions
1/2 cup apple cider vinegar
1/2 cup honey
1 tablespoon shoyu

Peel the onions and slice them thinly. Combine the vinegar, honey, and shoyu in a glass or ceramic bowl and add the sliced onions. Cover and refrigerate for at least 24 hours to allow onions to absorb maximum flavor.

The onions will keep in the refrigerator for about two weeks or longer. In fact, I keep mine going by adding more to it. All the ingredients are preservers so this zingy component can be kept at hand as a companion to many dishes.

Most refrigerators are filled with jars and packages of ready-made ingredients. My refrigerator is also filled with jars and containers of ready-made things, but mine are all labeled by hand, lending a personal touch most people haven't asked of their food. No salad, sandwich, or cracker will ever be boring if you keep these onions handy.

marinated white onion rings

74

Put all the ingredients in a bowl. Toss together, place in an airtight container, and refrigerate. They will keep up to a week.

1 medium-sized portobella mushroom, sliced

2 tablespoons olive oil

1 tablespoon shoyu

1 tablespoon water

1/2 teaspoon onion powder

1/2 teaspoon dried thyme

Keep Marinated Mushrooms on hand to top or to add savory depth to your central dishes. They work well on salads and in sandwiches and can be dehydrated to produce intense and versatile little morsels for various uses. They also make delicious picnic fare. Eating outdoors always makes me feel connected to nature so I picnic often. It's easy to pack up several delicacies along with hearts of romaine lettuce to use as scoops or wraps. A delightful picnic might include Marinated Mushrooms, Carrot Pâté, Cashew Cream Cheese, and Marinated White Onion Rings, along with fresh tomatoes, avocados, radish sprouts, and hearts of romaine lettuce.

marinated mushrooms

dehydrator

2 cups soaked walnuts
3/4 cup maple sugar
pinch of cinnamon
pinch of salt

Toss the walnuts with the maple sugar, cinnamon, and salt. Spread on a solid dehydrator sheet and dry at 105 degrees for 3 to 4 hours. Turn them, and dry completely, approximately 10 to 15 hours in total, though time will vary depending on climate and season. Store in a container with a lid.

This is one of those surprising components I keep on the side. A variety of textures are an important element in a truly superb offering. I have used these to accent everything from salads to desserts. They can be kept in the refrigerator or stored in the freezer. It will probably be necessary to hide them in a container labeled . . . "science experiment" . . . or something similar. Many a good soul has come to ruin over these tempters.

candied walnuts

When I give juicing classes, the question I hear most often is "what do I do with all this carrot pulp?" I once suggested composting, but have since discovered a myriad of uses for this raw material. This excellent cracker spread is one of my favorites and it is handy at a picnic.

food processor

2 cups carrot pulp

1 cup pine nuts

1 cup water

2 tablespoons almond butter

1/4 cup mellow white miso

3 to 5 cloves garlic

1 teaspoon dried thyme

1/2 teaspoon ground cumin

1/8 teaspoon cayenne

Put all the ingredients in a food processor and process until smooth. Refrigerate in an airtight container until ready to serve.

carrot pâté

4 red, yellow, or green sweet bell peppers

1 cup apple cider vinegar

1/2 cup honey

1/2 cup shoyu

1 teaspoon ground cumin

1 teaspoon dried thyme

1 teaspoon onion powder

1/8 teaspoon cayenne

4 to 6 cloves garlic

Remove stems and seeds from the peppers and cut them into strips or chunks. Place the vinegar, honey, shoyu, cumin, thyme, onion powder, cayenne, and garlic in a quart jar or similar glass container with a tight-fitting lid and shake until the honey dissolves. Add the pepper strips to the jar. Close the lid securely and refrigerate. Flavors will develop in about 4 hours, but the pickled peppers can be kept up to several weeks under refrigeration.

> I always have these in my refrigerator. They are just right on a sandwich or salad, or in any other dish that could use a little something extra. The manner in which they are prepared can be duplicated with any vegetable. It's alive, it's good, and it lasts.

pickled peppers

80

something good to drink

blender

Dice the mango and place it in a blender. (Dicing helps to eliminate stringiness if the mango has a fibrous texture.) Add the banana and orange juice and blend until smooth.

1 mango, peeled and cut from the stone

1 banana

3/4 cup orange juice

serves 1 or 2

I serve this anytime, with breakfast, lunch, or dinner, when mangoes are in season. Unlike the traditional version, this one is sweetened only with fruit. Make sure your mangoes are soft and fully ripe to ensure sweetness. The recipe can double as a dessert sauce or can be frozen into popsicles.

mango lassi

juicer

1/2 pound ginger root
1/2 cup honey
1/2 teaspoon cinnamon
1/4 teaspoon nutmeg
1/8 teaspoon powdered
green cardamom

Juice enough of the ginger root to produce 1/2 cup of juice. Add the honey and stir to dissolve. Mix in the cinnamon, nutmeg, and cardamom. Store in a glass jar in the refrigerator until needed. It will keep indefinitely.

To make a cup of Ginger Tonic Tea, place 1 tablespoon Ginger Tonic in a teacup, stir in 1/4 cup freshly squeezed lemon juice, and add warm water (110 degrees).

I rarely get sick, but I embrace the occasional cold as good housekeeping. This sassy little number will lessen your suffering and speed your recovery when you are a bit under the weather.

ginger tonic

84

gallon pitcher with lid

Place the fruit, vinegar, honey, and hibiscus flowers in a one-gallon container and fill with water. Cover with cheesecloth and let it sit in a warm spot for 2 or more days. Strain and refrigerate when it has reached your desired potency.

4 cups dried fruit (prunes, raisins, apricots, berries)

1/3 cup raw apple cider vinegar

1/2 cup raw honey

dried hibiscus flowers (look for them at the health food store)

pure water

A neighbor was telling me about the wine her grandmother made in her kitchen. I immediately went home and made my own version. Two days later I was enjoying my sparkling, new beverage. Naturally, the longer it sits the more fermentation. I prefer to drink mine before it develops a substantially intoxicating quality. Experiment and create; this recipe is a launching pad.

honey wine

juicer

handful of fresh cilantro
1 clove garlic
1 stalk celery
2 medium-sized cucumbers, peeled

serves 1 thirsty person

Put the cilantro and the garlic in the juicer first, followed by the celery and then the cucumber. Serve immediately.

You have probably heard the expression "cool as a cucumber." This is based in fact. The cucumber is high in minerals that keep us calm. This drink will keep you delightfully chilled out.

cool as a cucumber

This delicious, rich nut milk is easy to make. Make it in small batches; it is best when very fresh.

blender

nylon nut bag or very fine sieve for straining

1 cup soaked almonds

2 cups water

If you want to have almond milk first thing in the morning, it's handy to soak the almonds overnight. Otherwise, soak them 6 hours as for all dark nuts used in the recipes, or use almonds you have soaked in larger batches and have on hand. Rinse and drain. Place in a blender with the 2 cups of water. Blend well, then strain through a nut milk bag (see resources) or a very fine sieve.

almond milk

87

blender

nylon nut bag or very
fine sieve for straining

1 cup soaked almonds
1-1/2 cup water

Place almonds in the blender with the soaking water. Purée, then strain through a nut bag or a very fine sieve.

1/4 cup honey
1/2 teaspoon cinnamon
1/2 teaspoon vanilla

Return the strained mixture to the blender. Add the honey, cinnamon, vanilla, and ice cubes and purée until the desired thickness is achieved.

ice cubes

This is decadent nutrition,
pure and simple.

almond milkshake

88

desserts

Soak the flaxseed in 2 cups of water for 6 hours. It will absorb all the water. Combine the soaked flaxseed, honey, flaxmeal, 1 cup water, cinnamon, and vanilla in a food processor. Process for several minutes.

Remove mixture to a bowl and fold in the raisins by hand. Shape the dough into cookies and place on a dehydrator sheet. Dehydrate 6 hours on a Teflex sheet, then flip to a perforated sheet and continue to dehydrate 6 more hours. Eat them all.

2 cups golden flaxseed

2 cups water

1 cup honey

1 cup flaxmeal (made by grinding flaxseed in a coffee grinder or spice mill)

1 cup water

1 tablespoon cinnamon

1/2 teaspoon vanilla

1 cup Thompson seedless raisins

makes 12 cookies

> Before I travel, I make lots of these cookies to sustain my "rawness" while I'm out in the raw-unfriendly world. They travel well, keep well, taste great, and they deliver a happy energy buzz.

flaxmeal raisin cookies

food processor

2 cups soaked almonds
1/2 cup raw carob powder
1/2 cup honey
3 tablespoons almond butter
6 pitted dates
2 teaspoons cinnamon
1 teaspoon vanilla extract
1/2 teaspoon shoyu
1/8 teaspoon nutmeg

shredded organic coconut,
unpasteurized and unsulfured

makes about 20 pieces

Put the almonds, carob powder, honey, almond butter, dates, cinnamon, vanilla, shoyu, and nutmeg in a food process and thoroughly process until creamy.

Form the mixture into small balls. Roll each in coconut and place the finished candies in paper candy cups. Served either chilled or at room temperature.

Remember how much fun it was to lick the batter bowl? I pass this decadent feeling on to my friends and family by giving them chilled spoonfuls of this lovely concoction.

carob fudge

food processor
or Vita Mixer

1 cup soaked cashews
1/2 cup water
1/4 cup maple syrup
1/8 teaspoon nutmeg
1/4 teaspoon vanilla

1 cup frozen raspberries
1/2 cup maple syrup
1/2 teaspoon cinnamon

serves 3 to 4

Put the cashews, water, maple syrup, nutmeg, and vanilla in a food process and process until smooth. Transfer to another bowl.

Wash the processor bowl, then put the frozen raspberries, maple syrup, and cinnamon in it. Process until smooth.

Fill your chosen parfait glasses, alternately, with these two mixtures. Freeze until ready to serve.

I collect elegant glasses and build colorful desserts in them. Rather than trying to match everything, I go for variety. Raspberry parfait is an elegant presentation.

raspberry parfait

94

food processor
dehydrator

Put the apple, walnuts, pine nuts, sunflower seeds, maple sugar, carob powder, vanilla, shoyu, and nutmeg in a food processor and process to make a creamy dough.

1 golden delicious apple, peeled, cored, and diced

1 cup soaked walnuts

3/4 cup pine nuts

1/2 cup soaked sunflower seeds

1/2 cup maple sugar

1/4 cup raw carob powder

1 teaspoon vanilla extract

1/2 teaspoon shoyu

1/8 teaspoon nutmeg

Using a small scoop, form the dough into dome-shaped cookies and place on a dehydrator sheet.

Push two or three raspberries into the center of each cookie.

fresh raspberries

Dehydrate for 10 hours and then hide them in the back of the freezer.

makes 20 cookies

After you eat these delightfully soft, squishy cookies, your eyes will roll back in your head and you will hear yourself moan, "I can't believe it's raw!"

carob ooey-gooey cookies

95

Place the pecans, dates, cinnamon, and vanilla in a food processor. Pulse into dough. Press into a 7-inch springform pan.

Toss the apples with the cinnamon and lemon juice. Soften the apples in the dehydrator for 2 hours at room temperature or overnight in the refrigerator.

Put dates, maple syrup, and cinnamon in a blender and blend, adding just enough water so that mixture will turn easily.

Toss the apple mixture with the date paste and use the mixture to fill the pie shell. To serve, top with soaked raisins and try to divide evenly.

7-inch springform pan

1 cup soaked pecans
5 pitted dates
1/2 teaspoon cinnamon
3 drops vanilla

5 or 6 golden delicious apples, peeled, cored, and sliced thinly
1 teaspoon cinnamon
1-1/2 tablespoons freshly squeezed lemon juice

1 cup pitted dates
1/4 cup maple syrup
1 teaspoon cinnamon

My mother's apple pies were a great model for me. While developing this recipe, I meditated on all their seductive elements. The result was the incorporation of a spiced date paste that mimics the sugar-cinnamon ooze in a traditional pie. Try this with Macadamia Cream and never look back. (For Macadamia Cream, place 1/2 cup macadamia nuts, 2 tablespoons honey, a pinch of cinnamon, a drop of vanilla, and 1/4 cup water in the blender and whip smooth.)

apple pie

blender

3/4 cup water
1/2 cup almond butter
1/2 cup maple syrup
1/2 cup raw carob powder
1 teaspoon shoyu
1/2 teaspoon vanilla
1/4 teaspoon cinnamon

Combine all the ingredients in a blender and blend until smooth. Refrigerate.

> This syrup will keep longer than your resistance. It will transform any fruit into an elegant dessert. Keep it in a squeeze bottle to assist your painterly flair.

carob syrup

98

food processor
dehydrator

Mince the strawberries, place them in a bowl, and drizzle them with honey. Turn to coat.

Place the cashews, walnuts, water, dates, maple syrup, vanilla, cinnamon, and salt in a food processor and process to make a creamy dough.

Using a small scoop, form the dough into dome-shaped cookies and place on solid dehydrator sheets. Make a dent in the top of each dome with your thumb and fill with honeyed strawberries.

Dehydrate for 10 hours. Store refrigerated in an airtight container.

10 ounces fresh or frozen strawberries

honey

2 cups soaked cashews

2 cups soaked walnuts

1 cup water

6 pitted dates

1/2 cup maple syrup

1 teaspoon vanilla

1/2 teaspoon cinnamon

pinch of salt

makes about 20 cookies

These cookies will make your house smell nice and are so good for you that you can eat them at any time of day. Offer them for breakfast and you'll get an instant reputation for serving dessert for breakfast. I have friends who insist that these cookies are really jellyrolls.

strawberry shortcake cookies

99

nut butter machine or juicer
capable of homogenizing nuts

food processor

blender

8-inch springform pan

1 cup soaked walnuts

2 tablespoon minced dates

1/2 teaspoon cinnamon

Put the walnuts, dates, and cinnamon in a food processor and process until smooth. Press into the bottom of an 8-inch springform pan and set aside.

2 cups soaked cashews

1/2 cup maple syrup

1/2 cup water

1/2 teaspoon vanilla

pinch of cinnamon

pinch of salt

For the white layer, homogenize the cashews in a juicer or nut butter machine. Put the resulting cashew butter in a food processor with the maple syrup, water, vanilla, cinnamon, and salt. Process until smooth. For the red layer, place the strawberries, syrup, and cinnamon in a blender and blend until smooth.

10 ounces hulled strawberries

1/2 cup maple syrup

pinch of cinnamon

Assemble the cake into 4 layers on top of the crust. Spread half the white cashew mixture over the crust, follow with half the strawberry mixture, then the remaining white half and the remaining red half. Freeze solid in the freezer. To serve, cut with warm knife.

strawberry ice cream cake

organizing your raw life

ENJOYING five to nine servings of fruits and vegetables a day (the advice of nearly all health professionals) becomes an intense adventure when you add delicious sauces, marinades—and your imagination. But whether you are experimenting with a few raw dishes or are on a path to complete raw living, a few new tricks for planning and preparation will stand you in good stead.

When I worked as a guide for a historic museum, part of the talk I gave was intended to make people think about how vital it had been to plan ahead in earlier times. Today we live in a convenience-oriented world and many things are available to us at the spur of the moment. But sometimes our uses of the time we save may nurture us less than the tasks we avoided in order to save it.

Raw fooders think about time a little differently from the way that others do. Most enjoy being in the moment as they are handcrafting meals. Most also become masters of planning ahead. They learn to make mobile feasts. Whether for a trip across town or to distant lands, my small containers and little cooler always accompany me.

If organization and planning do not come easily to you, eating raw will encourage these skills—and thus can transform every part of your life. When you walk into your kitchen and don't see anything ripening, soaking, marinating, or dehydrating, just take a minute and start something!

103

For me, there is such a joy in the food. It makes me feel very connected with the responsibility of my life. I know it is possible to spend just a few hours and prepare the basics for a week's feasting. I have done that both for myself and for others.

Hiring a raw chef service is another solution. This isn't a bad idea for someone starting out, although, just like crawling babies, raw foodists will soon stand and walk for themselves. Joining or organizing a raw pot luck group is a great way to get new ideas and a variety of tastes.

I consider it essential to have treats stashed in the refrigerator or freezer (Strawberry Ice Cream Cake is a good example). You can be rolling along great with a raw food plan when suddenly a bump appears in your emotional highway. Instead seeking comfort in thoughtless food, reinforce your life with a raw treat. If you haven't stashed something homemade, dates and macadamia nuts are a quick solution.

Think in terms of tools rather than heat and don't let an opportunity pass that might offer a new toy for your toolkit. I have a free standing rack of machines in my kitchen. It's taken awhile to collect them, but each and every one has brought new life to my raw meals. You don't have to worry about having the most popular brand of the day—just get something that is reasonably priced. I have had good luck advertising for champion juicers and Vita-mixers. A friend who does the garage sale circuit says he sees Excalibur dehydrators and Cuisinart food processors all the time.

Last, keep your pantry stocked. Here's a quick checklist by food type. You might want to copy it and take it with you to the market.

a raw food pantry list

basics
apple cider vinegar
celtic sea salt
miso
olive oil
shoyo or tamari

fruits
dates
raisins

nuts and seeds
almonds
almond butter
cashews
flaxseed
macadamia nuts
pecans
pine nuts
sunflower seeds
tahini
walnuts

spices and herbs
basil
cayenne
chili powder
cinnamon
cumin
curry
garlic
nutmeg
onion powder
oregano
peppercorns
rosemary
sage
tarragon
thyme
turmeric

sweeteners
carob powder
honey
maple sugar
maple syrup

building a menu: the dinner party

WHEN EATING ON MY OWN, I tend to keep things simple. My meals will incorporate a sauce, a filling, or a marinade with currently available organic favorites. But raw food menus can be as elaborate or inventive as you are inclined to make them. The sample dinner party menu here is a model for composing any meal that will please family, friends, or yourself.

The first tip in menu planning to to be bold in mixing and matching components from one or more dishes to come up with your own new ideas. Keep some of the filling from the Raw Ravioli aside to spread on cucumber slices or use the Carrot Croquette recipe as a pâté for crackers rather than drying it into croquettes. In my raw food training sessions I teach concepts and components along with creative thinking. And don't forget—without fail, whatever you serve must be pleasing to the eye.

I love a grand dinner. Choosing to serve small portions in multiple courses over a leisurely hour or two will allow for the conversation and the communion that is one of life's dearest pleasures. Small courses also allow people to focus on the layers or notes of an offering. Each plate is prepared like a painting, creating elegance and encouraging meditation. Far more than physical nourishment, this is a celebration of life itself.

While it is true that a raw diet will enhance your physical beauty, it will also awaken a higher vibration of your spirit. My favorite benefit of raw cuisine is that as the years pass it can help you remain comfortable in your body. I don't want to stop old age. I want to reinvent it. Age is wisdom. If we can hold the wisdom without the pain of aging, this will be a new world.

sample menu

first course

Baby radicchio cups in tomato salsa broth with a shower of lemon zest

Start by reducing the Festive Radicchio recipe to half. Make tomato salsa broth by reducing the Gazpacho recipe to half, then ladle it into wide, shallow bowls. Fill the small inner leaves of the raddicchio head as directed for the recipe and arrange them in the broth. Crown the dish with a shower of finely grated lemon rind.

second course

A nest of zucchini noodles tossed in Alfredo sauce and served in a ring of pickled vegetables

This is the Alfredo recipe arranged with a variety of colorful vegetables that have been marinating in the Pickled Pepper vinaigrette.

third course

Walnut raviolis caressed by a savory carrot almond sauce

Make the Raw Ravioli recipe for this course.

fourth course

Portobella mushroom fillets with red pepper fingers

Double the sauce from the Mushroom, Lettuce, and Tomato Sandwich recipe, add strips from one red bell pepper and a few slivers of white onion, and use this to marinate two large portobella mushrooms (remove the dark feathered underside and slice them into

long strips before marinating).
Warmed in the dehydrator for 20
minutes before serving.

finishing course

**Almond fudge mousse, crowned
with macadamia cream sauce and
drizzled with strawberry coulis.**

To make the mousse, use the
Carob Syrup recipe, cutting the
shoyu down to a few drops and
adding only enough water to
allow the mixture to turn in the
blender. Layer in cocktail glasses
with macadamia cream (find it at
the end of the Apple Pie recipe)
and chill until serving.
Strawberry coulis is just a
combination of strawberries,
maple syrup, and a splash of
water, whirled in the blender.

Suggested Reading

Fit for Life, by Harvey and Marilyn
Diamond (Warner Books)

Don't Drink Your Milk, by Dr. Frank A.
Oski M.D. (Teach Services)

Diet for a New America, by John
Robbins (H J Kramer)

The Food Revolution, by John Robbins
(Conari Press)

Bragg Healthy Lifestyle, by Paul Bragg
N.D. and Patricia Bragg N.D. (Health
Science)

Survival into the Twenty-First Century, by
Viktoras Kulvinskas (Twenty-First
Century Publications)

Hooked on Raw, by Rhio (Beso
Entertainment)

Conscious Eating, by Gabriel Cousens
M.D. (North Atlantic Books)

The Miracle of Fasting, by Paul Bragg
N.D. and Patricia Bragg N.D. (Decapolis
Books)

Rational Fasting, by Arnold Ehret
(Benedict Lust Publications)

The Raw Life, by Paul Nison (343
Publishing Company)

Love Your Body, by Viktoras Kulvinskas

The Sunfood Diet Success System, by
David Wolfe (Maul Brothers Publishing)

Eating for Beauty, by David Wolfe (Maul
Brothers Publishing)

index

Chef Suzanne Alex Ferrara is an artist, chef, and yoga instructor. She was born in Berkeley, California, and currently lives in Little Rock, Arkansas. In 2001, she was part of the original development team for the reknowned raw food restaurant Roxanne's in Larkspur, California.

Chef Alex honed her food skills as owner and manager of a juice bar and restaurant, purveyor of a natural food store, and head of her own vegetarian/vegan cooking school. She has catered for Caribbean sailboat cruises, consulted on recipes for specialty restaurants, and written a weekly food column featuring vegetarian and vegan recipes.

She has also exhibited her sculptures and paintings in New York, Florida, New Mexico, and California, and her work is collected internationally. As an artist she brings her love of vibrant color to the raw food table.

———————————————

Wildcat Canyon, a division of Council Oak Books, LLC, publishes books that embrace such subjects as friendship, spirituality, women's issues, home and family, all with a focus on self-help and personal growth. Great care is taken to create books that inspire reflection and improve the quality of our lives. Our books invite sharing and are frequently given as gifts.

For more information about Wildcat Canyon or Council Oak titles, please contact:

Council Oak Books

2105 East Fifteenth Street, Suite B

Tulsa, Oklahoma 74104

918.743.BOOK

order@counciloakbooks.com